THIS BOOK BELONGS TO:

....

© AL-AQSA PUBLISHERS 2011

Reprint 2021

Al-Aqsa Publishers
P.O. Box 5127
Leicester
LE2 0WU

E-mail: info@aqsa.org.uk | Website: www.aqsa.org.uk

Illustrated by Ghazala Caratella

Design and Layout by Shoayb Adam

With special thanks to Sanam Mirza

The Prophets in Palestine

Prophet 'Isa عَلَيْهِ السَّلَام

Over two thousand years ago something incredible happened in Jerusalem which changed the world. A great prophet was born.

The Prophet was called 'Isa ﷺ and this is the story of his life.

The mother of 'Isa ﷺ was called Mariam and she was a very special person and one of the best women on earth.

Allah ﷻ was very pleased with her. There is a Surah in the Quran which is named after her, called Surah Mariam.

سورة مريم

Mariam's mother was called Hannah and her father was called Imran. Before Mariam was born, Hannah did not have any children and this made her very sad.

One day Mariam's mother saw a bird feeding its chicks and this made her want her own baby.

She prayed to Allah ﷻ to give her a righteous child.

Hannah made a promise to Allah ﷻ that if she had a baby she would put the child in the service of Masjid al-Aqsa.

Allah ﷻ answered her prayers and Hannah gave birth to a baby whom she called Mariam.

Hannah was worried about her promise to Allah ﷻ because at that time girls were not allowed to go into the sanctuary of Masjid al-Aqsa.

When Mariam was a little girl, Hannah took her to Masjid al-Aqsa. The imam there was Zakaria ﷺ who was also a prophet of Allah ﷻ. Zakaria ﷺ was married to Hannah's sister and was Mariam's uncle.

Zakaria ﷺ built Mariam a small room joining the main Masjid, and Mariam was allowed to stay in the compound of Masjid al-Aqsa. Mariam was a very pious girl and she spent her days worshipping Allah ﷻ and praying.

It is mentioned in the Qur'an that Mariam was the best of all the women in the world.

Mariam was not an ordinary person and she was blessed by Allah ﷻ. Whenever Zakaria عليه السلام would visit her room, he noticed that she always had fresh fruit which were normally out of season.

Zakaria عليه السلام once asked Mariam, 'Where did you get these fruits from?'

Mariam said, 'They are from Allah ﷻ. He provides for whoever He wants to.'

When Zakaria عليه السلام saw the favours of Allah سبحانه وتعالى on Mariam, he also prayed to Allah سبحانه وتعالى. Zakaria عليه السلام did not have any children of his own and both he and his wife were very old.

But when he saw that Allah سبحانه وتعالى can provide anything and everything, he asked Allah سبحانه وتعالى to give him a son. Allah سبحانه وتعالى accepted his prayer and his wife gave birth to a son.

Allah ﷻ also told Zakaria ﷺ to name him Yahya, which he did.

Yahya was the cousin of Mariam.

The dua of Zakaria ﷺ was accepted in Masjid al-Aqsa and everyone who visits there also hopes that when they pray in Masjid al-Aqsa their duas are also accepted.

Mariam was loved by everyone. All the children around Masjid al-Aqsa loved to be with her.

All the adults knew that she was righteous and that she was devoted to worshipping Allah ﷻ and they were fond of her.

One day while Mariam was praying in her room, a man appeared in front of her. Mariam became very scared and tried to run away.

The man explained to her that he was an angel sent by Allah ﷻ and that she did not need to worry. He explained that he came with a message and some good news from Allah ﷻ.

The angel said 'Allah ﷻ has sent me to tell you that you will be giving birth to a righteous son.'

Mariam was very worried and she explained to the angel that she was not married. How could she have a child without having a husband?

The angel reassured her and told her not to worry.

Allah ﷻ wanted her to have the child without a father and her son would be a sign for all people.

The news about having a child caused Mariam great worry. When the time arrived for the baby to be born, Mariam left Masjid al-Aqsa and Jerusalem.

She wondered in the desert heat and rested under a date palm tree.

Mariam was very worried about what would happen to her. But she heard a voice saying, 'Do not worry. Allah ﷻ has provided a stream for you to drink from. And if you shake the date tree, the fruit will fall which you can eat.'

Mariam followed the instructions and she had water to drink and ate dates from the tree.

Here, under the date palm, she gave birth to her son.

30

Mariam was very happy to see her son and Allah ﷻ instructed her to name him 'Isa ﷺ.

She took 'Isa and went back to Masjid al-Aqsa in Jerusalem. Mariam knew the people there would be surprised to see her with a baby.

She was commanded by Allah ﷻ not to speak to the people. When the people asked her what had happened, Mariam pointed towards the baby. The people were confused and said, 'How can we speak with a baby?'

Then a miracle occured. The baby back spoke to the people!

He said, 'I am a servant of Allah ﷻ. He has made me a prophet. He has told me to pray to Him and give charity to the poor. He has also told me to love my mother.'

The people were shocked.

When they heard a new born baby speak they accepted that this was a miraculous birth and that he was very special.

'Isa عليه السلام grew up in and around Jerusalem.

Even when he was a boy, he started preaching to the people to be good and honest, and to obey Allah تعالى.

He told them to help each other and not to fight.

When 'Isa ﷺ grew up, he travelled all over Palestine and he taught people to believe in Allah ﷻ.

But the people of the time were very cruel and arrogant. They refused to believe 'Isa ﷺ and asked him to prove that he was a prophet. 'Isa ﷺ prayed to Allah ﷻ for help.

Allah ﷻ helped 'Isa ﷺ by giving him very special powers to perform miracles.

'Isa ﷺ performed many miracles so that people would believe in Allah ﷻ.

He told them that all of these miracles were only possible by the power of Allah ﷻ and everybody must believe in Allah ﷻ.

But the people continued to ignore his message.

40

The Qur'an teaches us that there were special miracles performed by 'Isa ﷺ. One of them was curing people who were sick.

There were some people in Palestine who were suffering from a disease called leprosy which made their bodies rot away. No doctors could help them and there was no medicine to make them better. 'Isa ﷺ was given the power from Allah ﷻ to make them better and when he put his hands on them they recovered straight away.

There were also blind people who wanted to be cured. Allah ﷻ again provided 'Isa ﷺ with a special power and when he put his hands on their eyes they were cured and could see clearly.

Curing the diseases was not enough for some people who still did not believe that 'Isa عليه السلام was a prophet. They asked 'Isa عليه السلام for more proof to show that he was a prophet.

'Isa عليه السلام took some clay and shaped it like a bird. He than breathed onto the clay bird and with Allah's عز وجل power it came to life and flew away.

Some people then accused 'Isa ﷺ of using magic to perform the miracles and would not believe the clear signs sent by Allah ﷺ.

They asked him to bring the dead back to life if he was a prophet. Allah ﷺ helped Isa ﷺ and in front of everybody he brought one dead person back to life.

There were some believers who accepted everything 'Isa عليه السلام told them about Allah سبحانه وتعالى and the life after this world.

But some people refused to believe him and became his enemies.

They finally asked 'Isa عليه السلام to prove that he was a prophet by telling them what they had eaten and what food was in their stomachs. They also asked him to tell them what food they had in their houses.

Again Allah سبحانه وتعالى gave 'Isa عليه السلام the power to answer all of these questions correctly.

When 'Isa ﷿ realised that the people did not believe him except for a few, he turned to these believers and said to them, 'Who will help me in Allah's ﷻ cause?'

The people who believed him were called his disciples and they responded by saying, 'We will be Allah's ﷻ helpers because we believe in Allah ﷻ.'

The disciples said that they believed in the message brought by 'Isa ﷿ and that they would follow him.

'Isa ﷿ with his disciples continued teaching people about being good and honest, and to love Allah ﷻ and all his creation.

The disciples once asked 'Isa ﷺ for a special favour to help them become stronger believers.

They wanted Allah ﷻ to send down a feast from heaven so that they could eat it and this would help them to believe more strongly in Allah ﷻ. 'Isa ﷺ told them to fear Allah ﷻ and he did not want to pray for this.

However, when they asked again he prayed to Allah ﷻ for the feast.

Allah ﷻ sent down a table with amazing heavenly food for the disciples to eat.

The disciples witnessed the miracle of the food and they ate from it. There could be no doubt about the existence of Allah ﷻ and about 'Isa ﷺ being a prophet after this.

Allah ﷻ said 'Anyone who does not believe in Allah ﷻ after eating this meal will be punished with a punishment which no one else has ever seen before.'

This great event is mentioned in the Quran.

The people who believed in 'Isa ﷺ were mainly poor and few in numbers.

Despite this 'Isa ﷺ continued to preach from house to house and village to village throughout Palestine. He preached during the day and night. Because he spent all his time telling people about Allah ﷻ and about their religion, he never had a house and 'Isa ﷺ never got married.

The enemies of 'Isa ﷺ started getting worried as more people started listening to 'Isa ﷺ and accepting him as a prophet.

They thought 'Isa ﷺ would become more powerful than them. They started making evil plans and wanted to kill him.

At the time when 'Isa عليه السلام was alive, the Romans controlled the city of Jerusalem. Some people in Jerusalem went to the Roman king and told him lies about 'Isa عليه السلام.

They told him that 'Isa عليه السلام was going to take over the city and that he was a dangerous person.

They asked the Roman governor of Jerusalem who was called Pontius Pilate to kill 'Isa عليه السلام.

Pontius called for 'Isa ﷺ to be arrested and that 'Isa ﷺ be brought to him.

Allah ﷻ, through the angels informed 'Isa ﷺ of the plans made by his enemies.

'Isa ﷺ gathered all his disciples together and informed them about the plans to kill him. He did not ask them to protect him but instead asked them to carry on teaching people about Allah ﷻ.

All of the disciples immediately said that they would continue to work for Allah ﷻ.

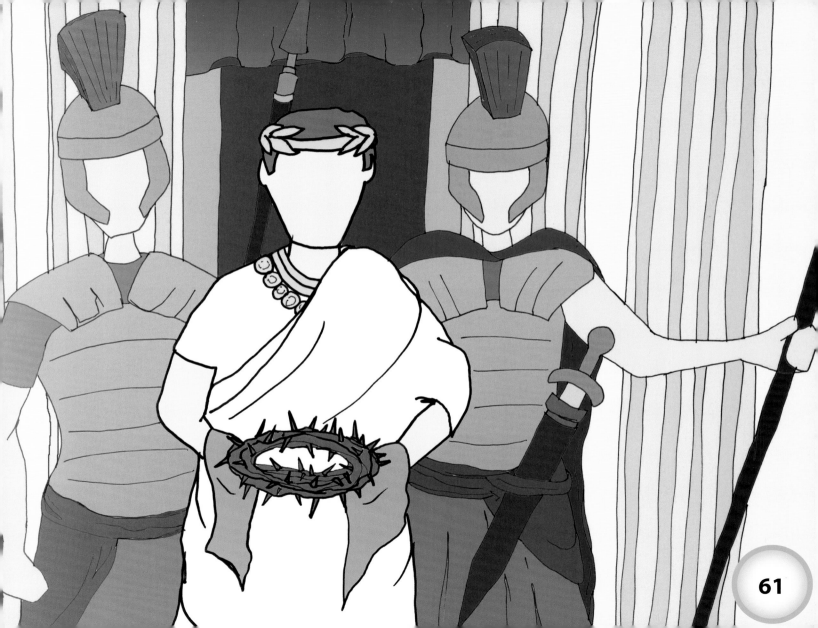

One night when 'Isa عليه السلام was alone, the enemies gathered around his house and wanted to kidnap him and take him to Pontius Pilate.

In the Quran, Allah سبحانه وتعالى says that the disbelievers planned to kill 'Isa عليه السلام but that Allah سبحانه وتعالى also had a plan and Allah سبحانه وتعالى is the best of planners.

They planned to kill 'Isa ﷺ by stretching his hands out and nailing them to a wooden crucifix.

This was a cruel punishment which happened at that time. However, before they could kill 'Isa ﷺ Allah ﷻ took 'Isa ﷺ away from Jerusalem by raising him up to heaven. Another person was made to look like 'Isa ﷺ and he was killed instead.

Allah ﷻ says in the Quran, 'They did not kill 'Isa ﷺ and they did not crucify him. It was just made to look like they did.'

When 'Isa ﷺ was taken up to heaven by Allah ﷻ, this was a unique event. It was like the miracle of his birth. He did not die on earth like every other human being before or after him.

He is now in Jannah and will one day return to earth when Allah ﷻ decides. This will happen towards the end of time when Muslims will be facing very hard times. When he returns, he will bring peace to earth.

67

The story of 'Isa ﷺ tells us how important Jerusalem and Masjid al-Aqsa is. Mariam, the mother of 'Isa ﷺ, lived in Masjid al-Aqsa and spent her time praying to Allah ﷻ.

'Isa ﷺ was born close to Jerusalem and he spent many years in the city teaching people about Allah ﷻ. Finally, it was from Jerusalem that 'Isa ﷺ was raised to heaven by Allah ﷻ.

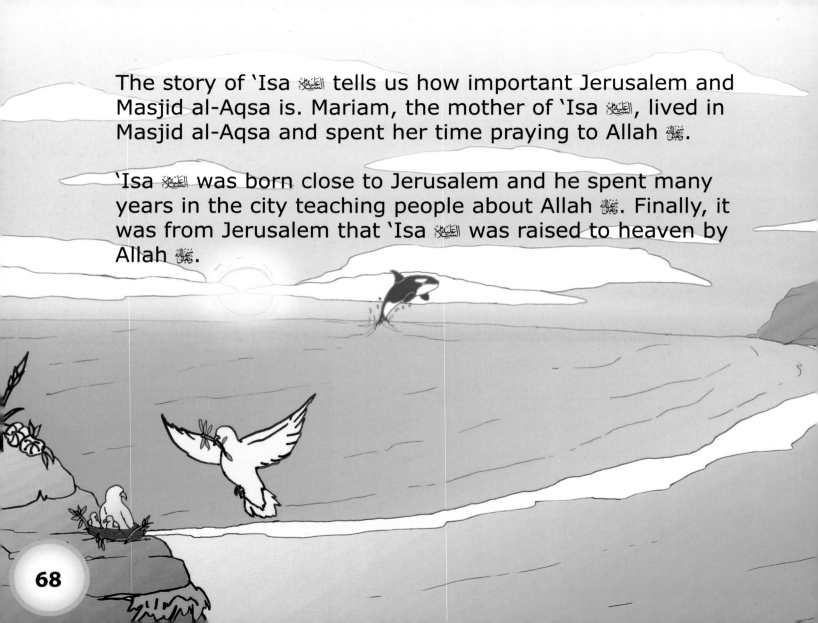